DRAW SUPER MANGA!

DAVID OKUM

IMPACT
CINCINNATI, OHIO
www.impact-books.com

How to Use This Book

There are three or four steps for each drawing.

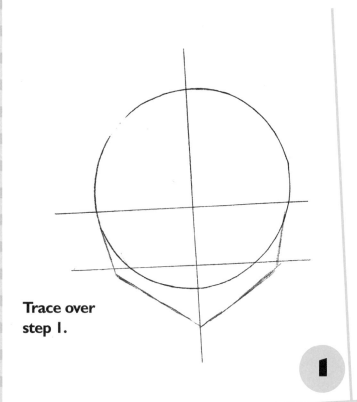

Trace over step 1.

1

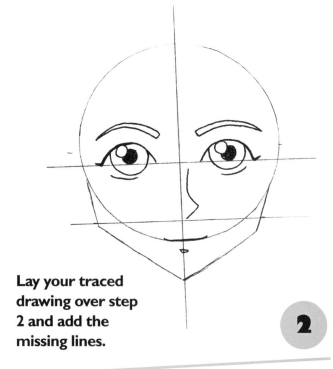

Lay your traced drawing over step 2 and add the missing lines.

2

For step 3, add the details and erase the extra lines.

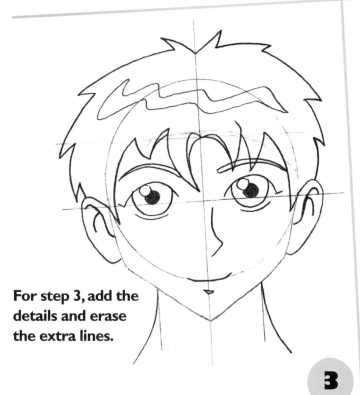

3

Darken the important lines on the last step and you're finished!

4

Shapes

Everything is made up of four main shapes: circles, squares, rectangles and triangles.

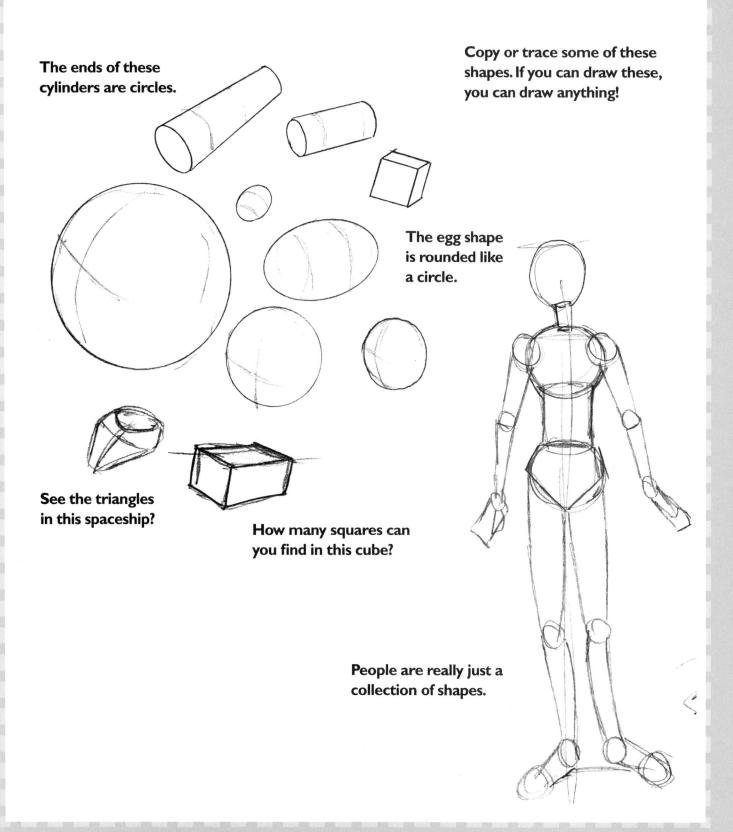

The ends of these cylinders are circles.

Copy or trace some of these shapes. If you can draw these, you can draw anything!

The egg shape is rounded like a circle.

See the triangles in this spaceship?

How many squares can you find in this cube?

People are really just a collection of shapes.

Shapes for Cars and Spaceships

Draw the shapes that make up the cars and spaceships.

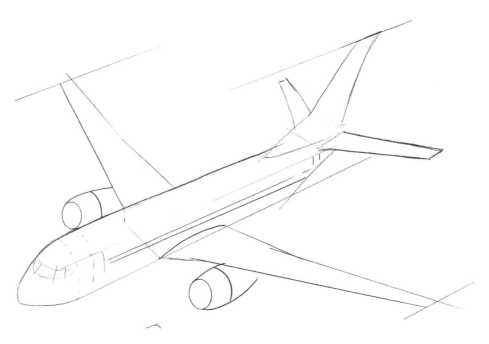

Look for the triangles and circles in this jet. Draw or trace it using as few lines as you can.

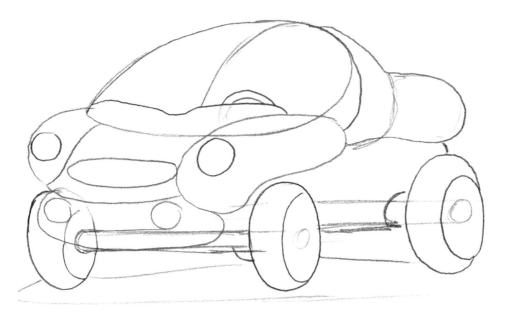

Remember the shapes and have fun coming up with your own strange cars and spaceships.

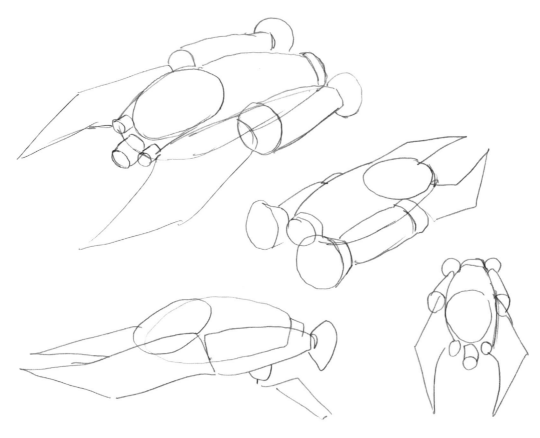

You can draw all kinds of spaceships
with basic shapes.

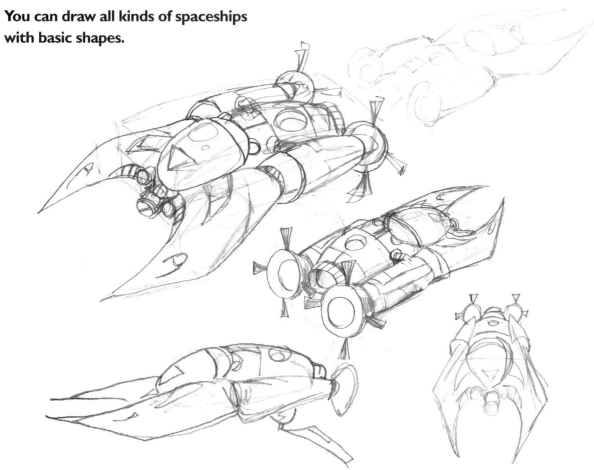

Drawing Eyes

Eyes are made up of circles inside circles....

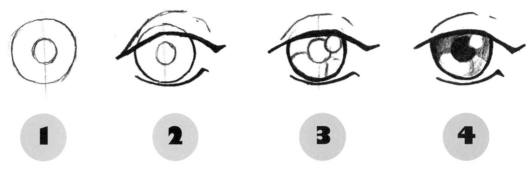

1 2 3 4

....or ovals inside ovals.

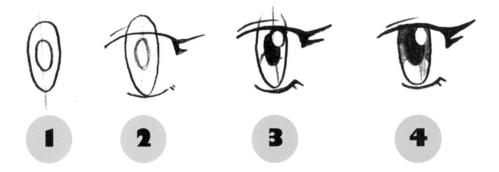

1 2 3 4

You can draw manga eyes almost any way you like.

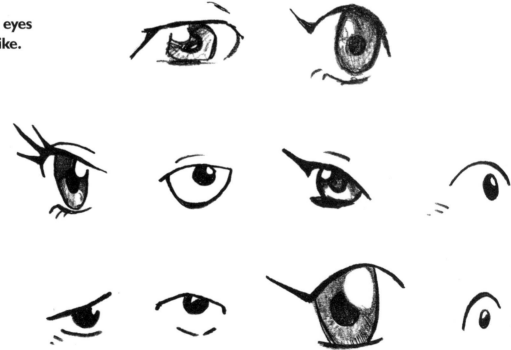

Drawing Pairs of Eyes

Eyes come in pairs. Use the guidelines to help you line them up.

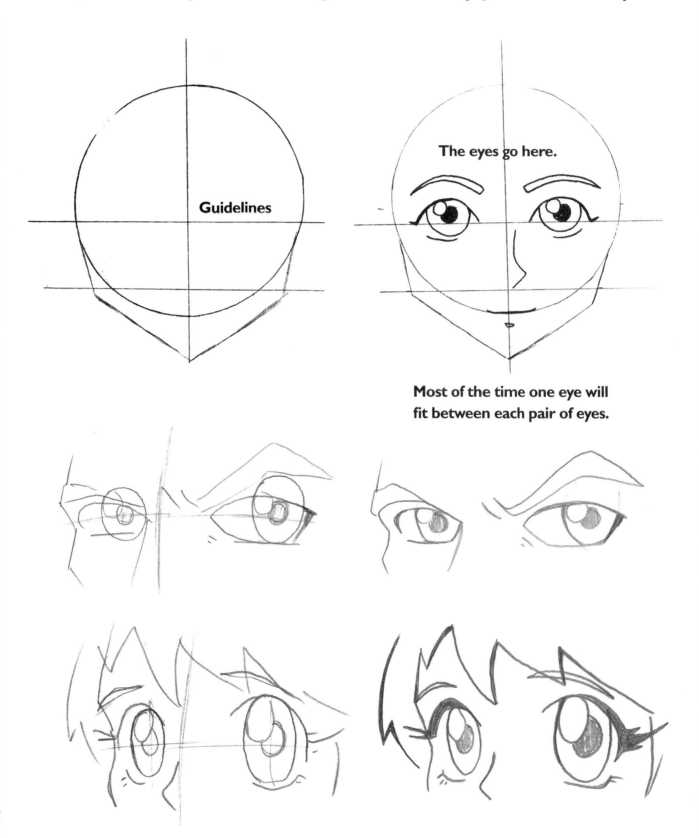

Guidelines

The eyes go here.

Most of the time one eye will
fit between each pair of eyes.

Drawing Hair

Draw hair in clumps or chunks.

Copy or trace the clumps of hair

Types of Hair

Manga hair shows manga personality. The wilder the character, the wilder the hair.

Face, Sideview

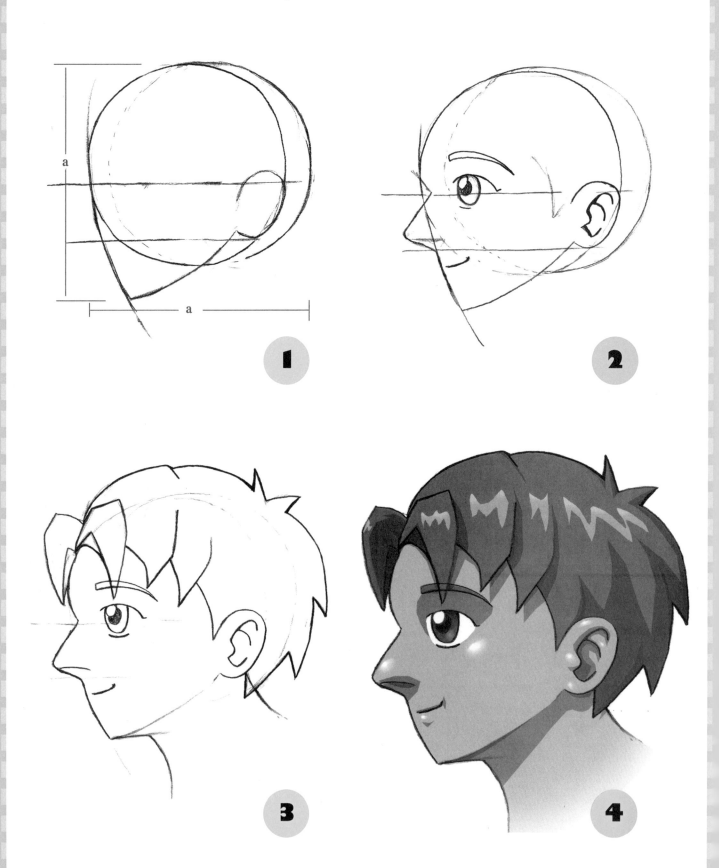

Face, 3/4-View

How Many Heads Tall Are You?

When we say that most adults are 7 to 8 heads tall, we mean if you stacked 7 to 8 adult heads on top of each other they would be as tall as one adult. And that's not all you can figure out using heads!

Adults are from 7 to 8 heads tall.

Eyes are small.

Shoulders are about 2 heads wide.

The neck is about ¼ of a head.

Hands are about the size of the face from chin to eyebrows.

Legs and feet take up half of the total body.

Adults

Teens range from 7 to 7½ heads tall.

Large eyes.

Eyes are smaller
for tired or really
smart teens.

Shoulders are
about 1½ to 2
heads wide.

Large hands
and feet.

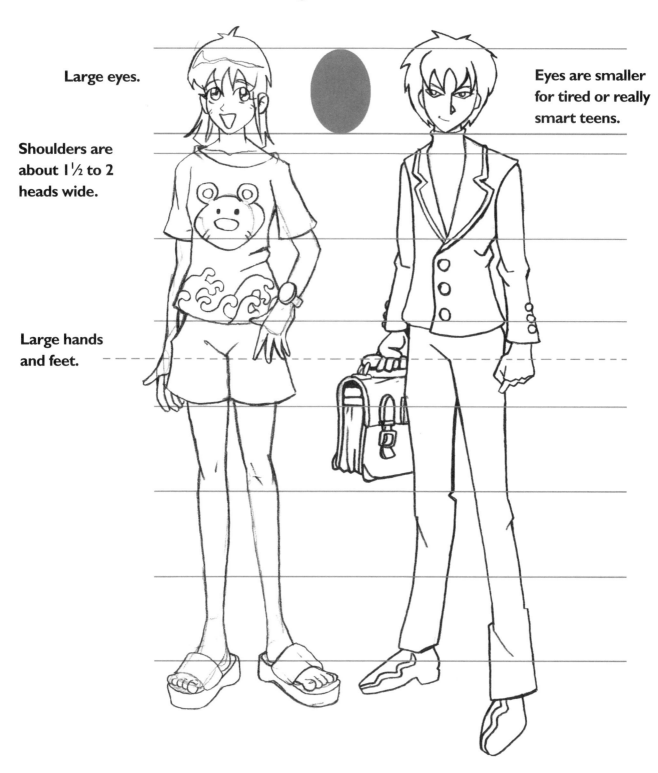

Teens

Kids are 4½ to 5 heads tall.

Shoulders are 1 head wide or smaller.

Feet, legs and waist should be ½ the total height.

Kids

Chibis are 2½ to 3 heads tall.

Eyes take up ⅓ of the head.

Head, feet and hands are huge.

The Chibi

The SD is 2 heads tall.

Eyes take up no less than ⅓ of the head.

No nose!

Small hands with fat fingers or no fingers at all.

Simple feet.

Super-Deformed

Drawing Hands

Hands start with shapes just like everything else.

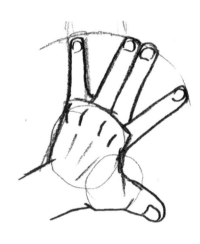

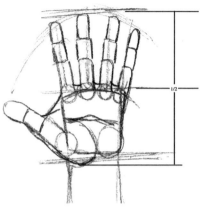

The longest finger is about the same size as the palm.

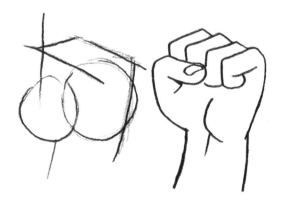

Draw your own hand. Pick up something and draw your hand holding it.

Drawing Feet

Look at the shapes in feet!

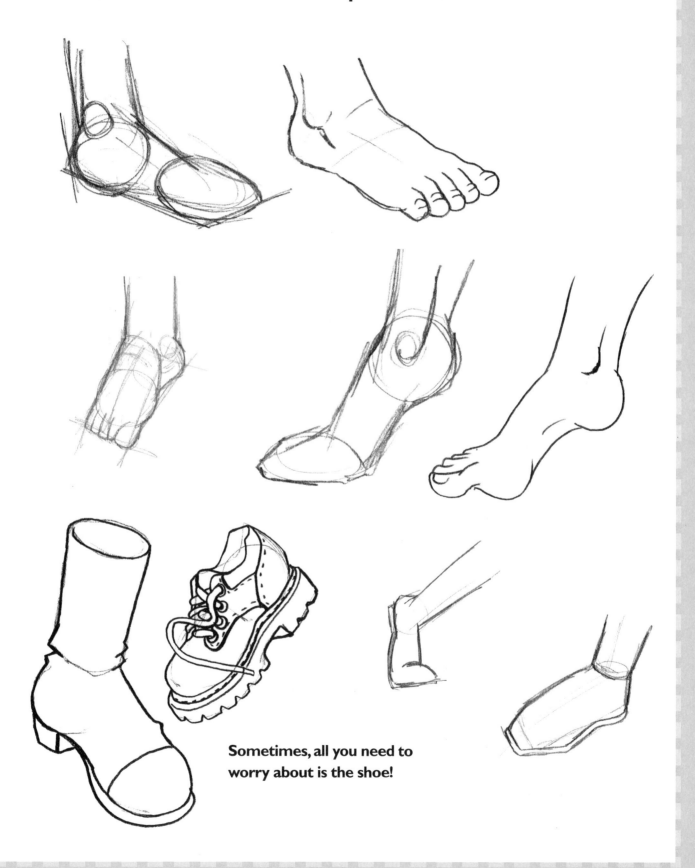

Sometimes, all you need to worry about is the shoe!

Clothes

Clothes can be tricky. Here are some tips to help you.

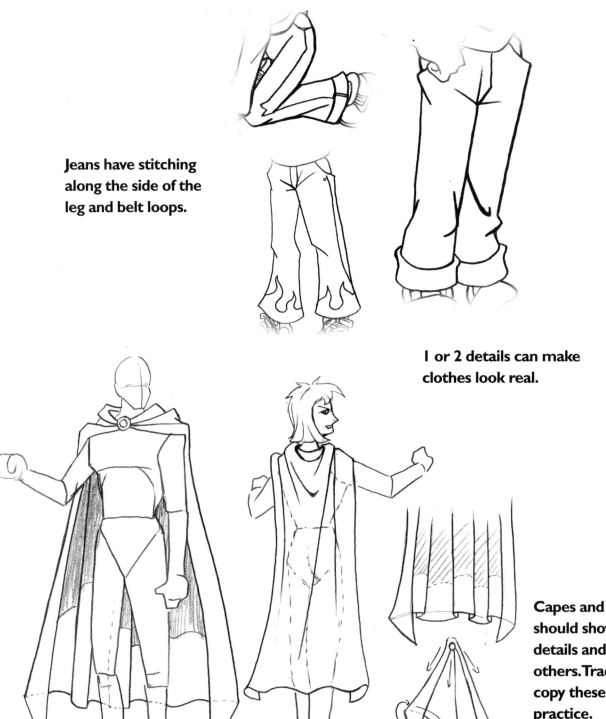

Jeans have stitching along the side of the leg and belt loops.

1 or 2 details can make clothes look real.

Capes and dresses should show some details and hide others. Trace or copy these for practice.

Manga girls wear different school uniforms. Many girls wear very baggy socks as well as hair clips, purses and school bags.

Boys' uniforms have dark pants and jackets.

Chibi

4

The Mascot

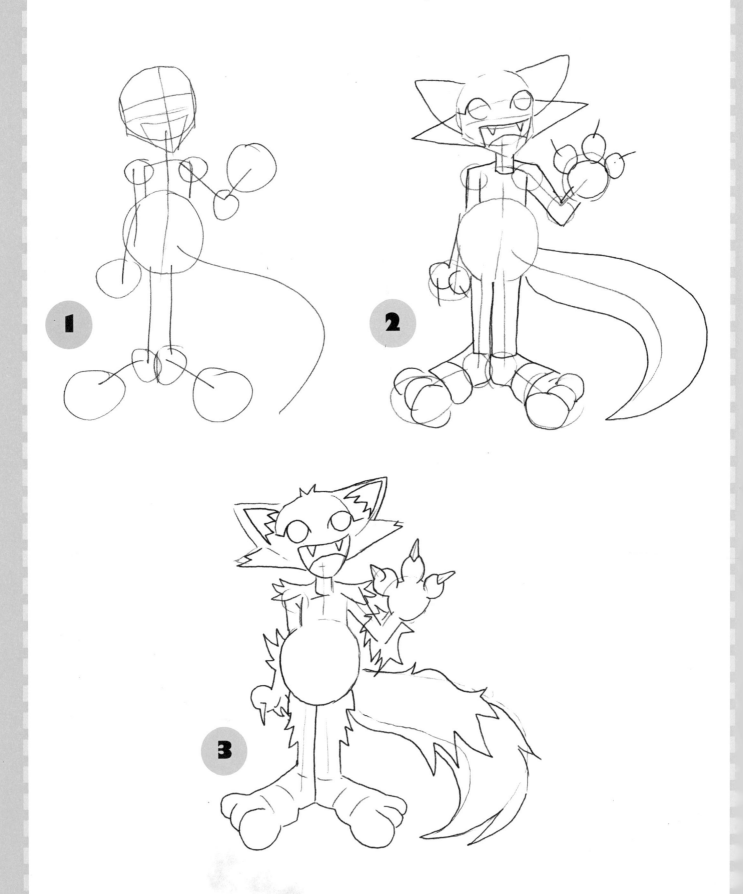

4

The Kid

4

Magical Girl

4

Main Hero

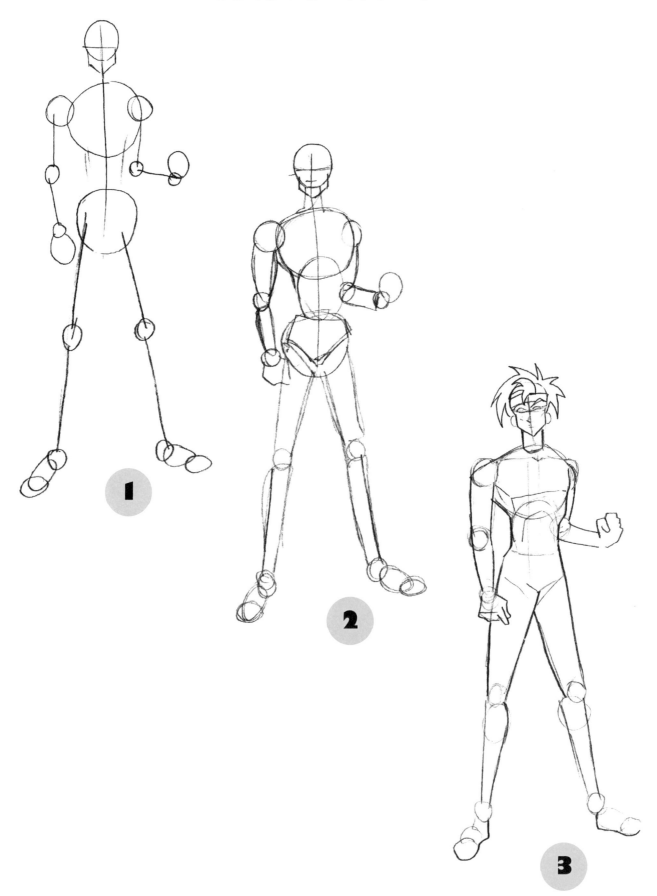

4

Rebel Hero

4

The Big Guy

4

Mascot Pet

Pretty Girl

Fallen Hero

4

Evil Queen

The Big Bad Guy

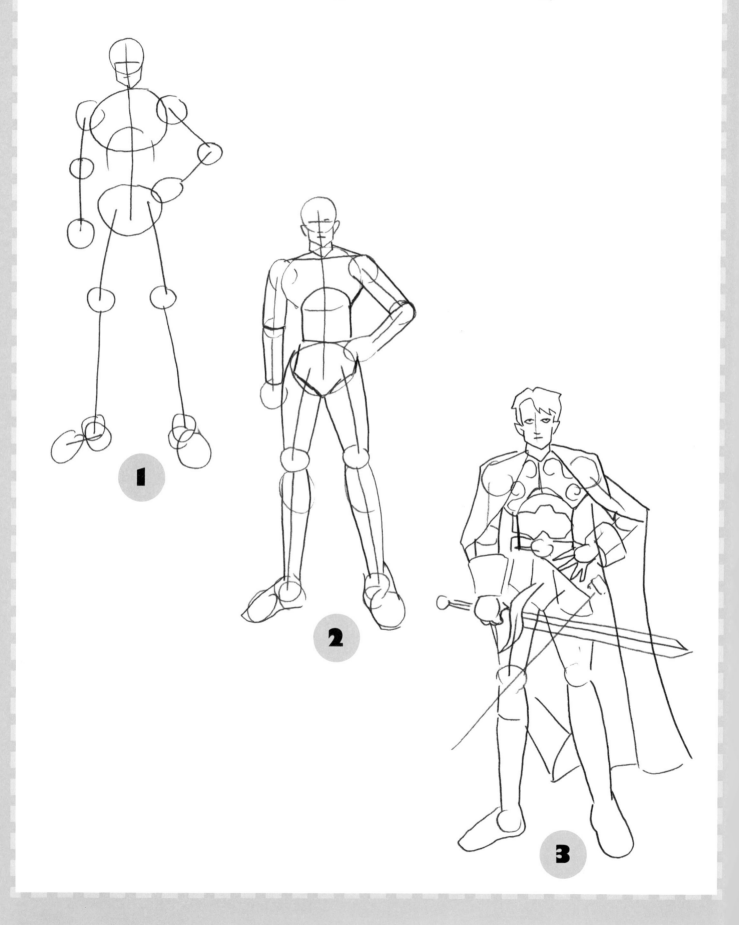

4

The Goon

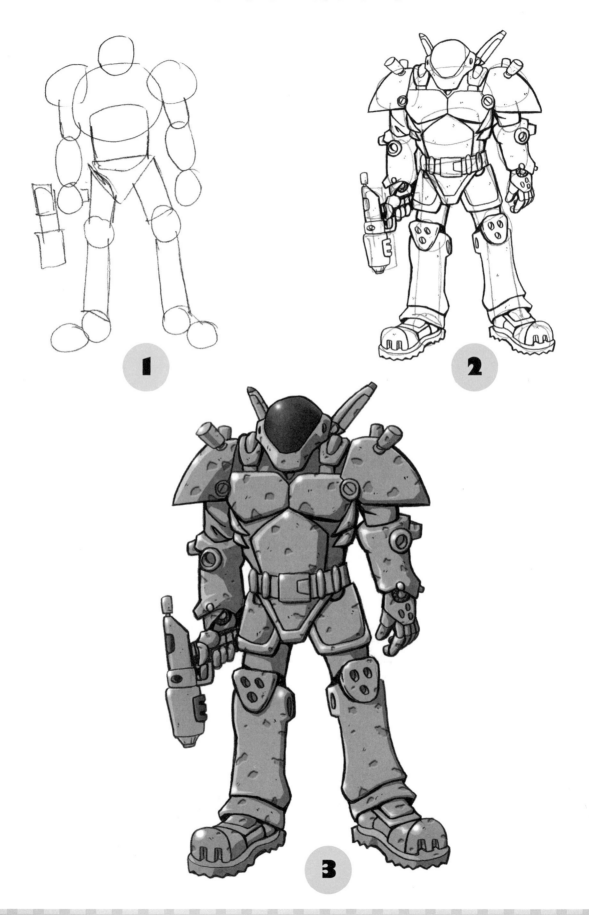

The Fiend

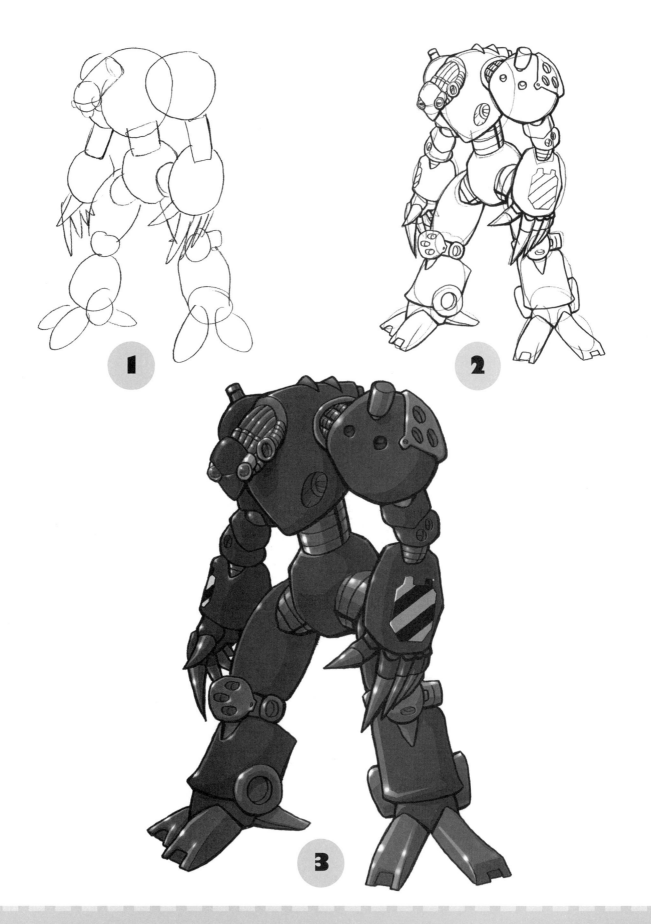

Boy Martial Artist

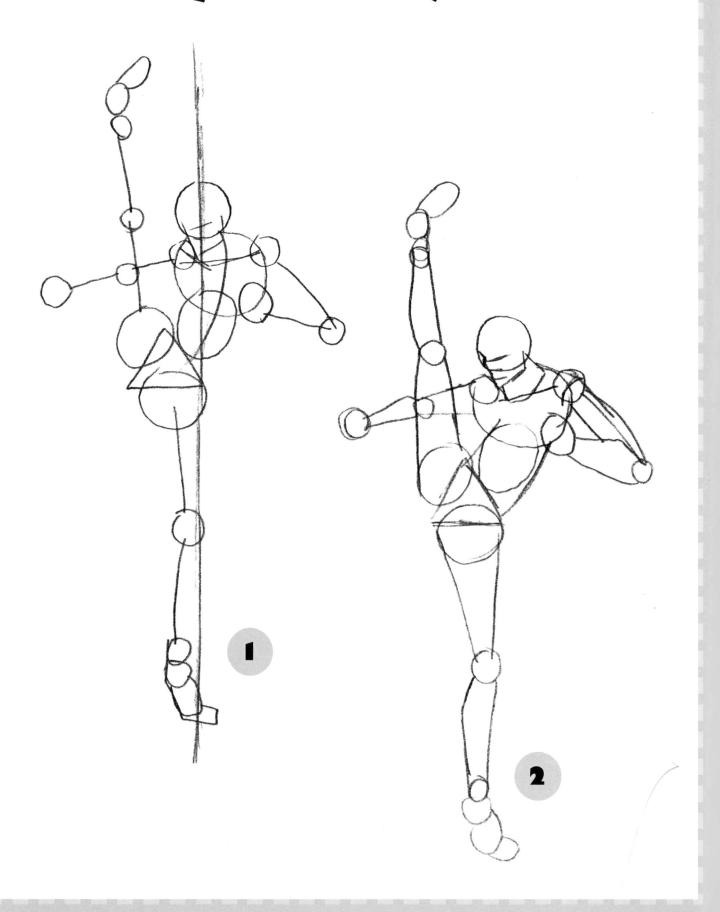

3

Girl Martial Artist

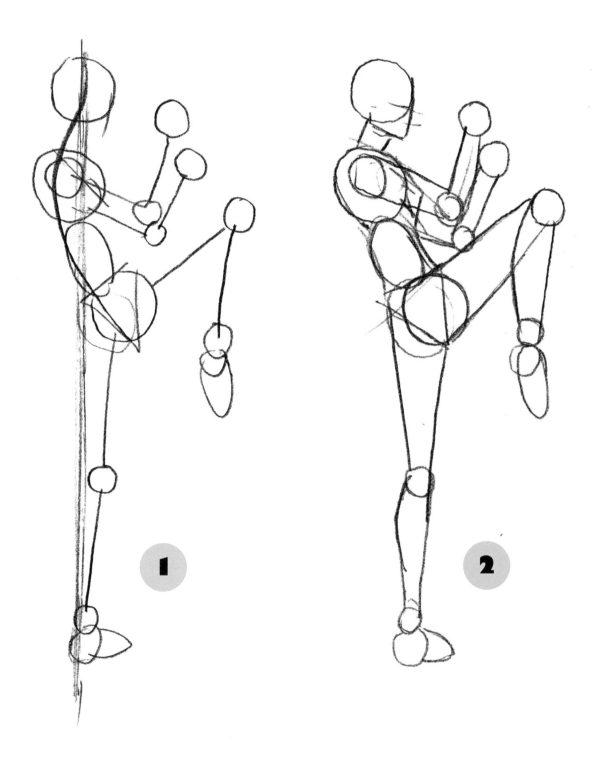

1

2

3

Mecha

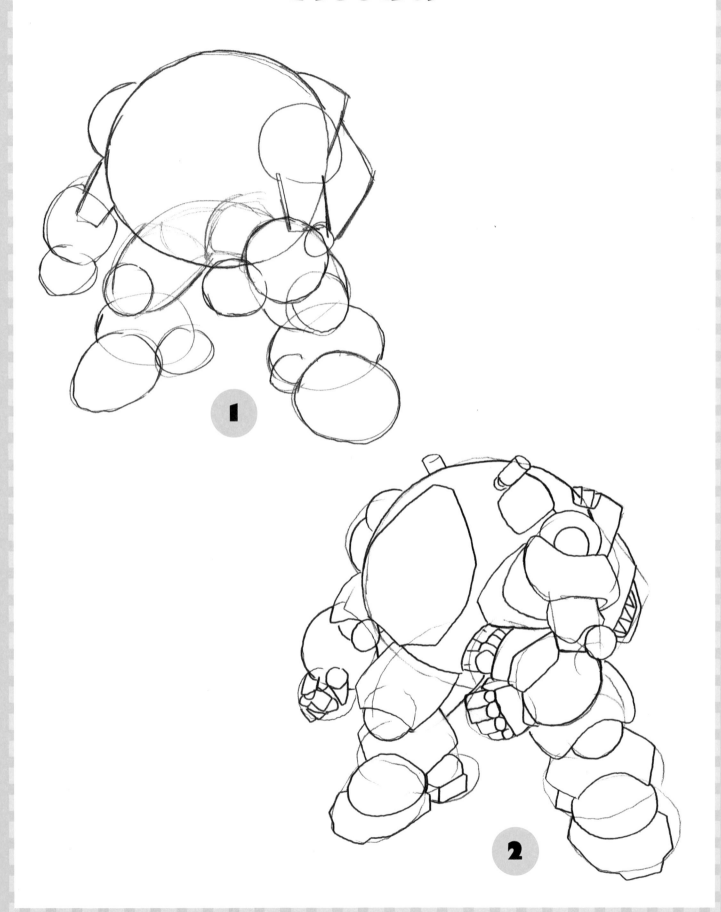

Crab Bot

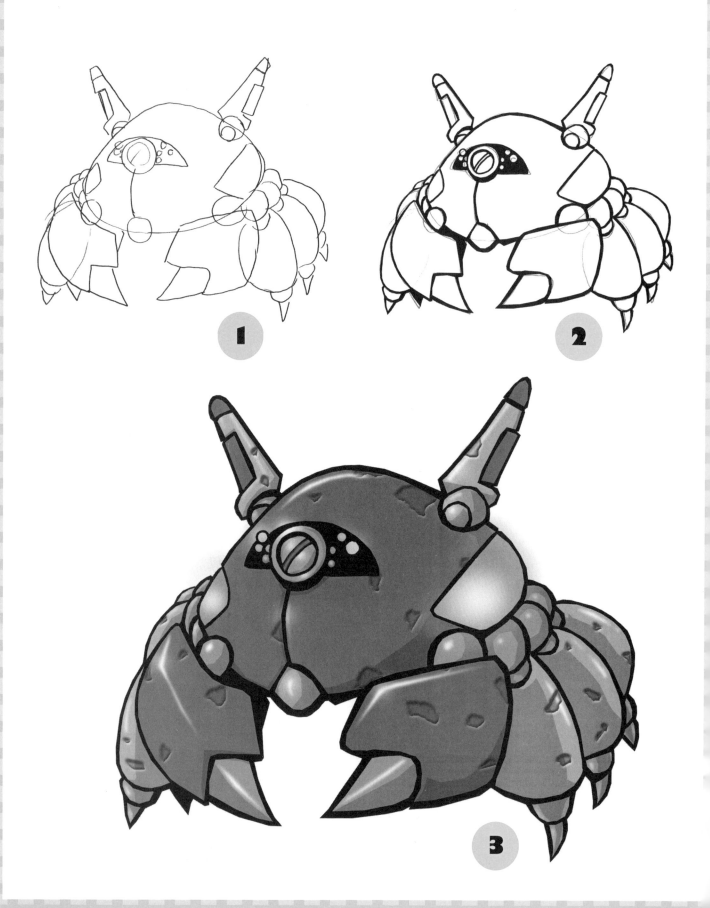

Humanoid Robot

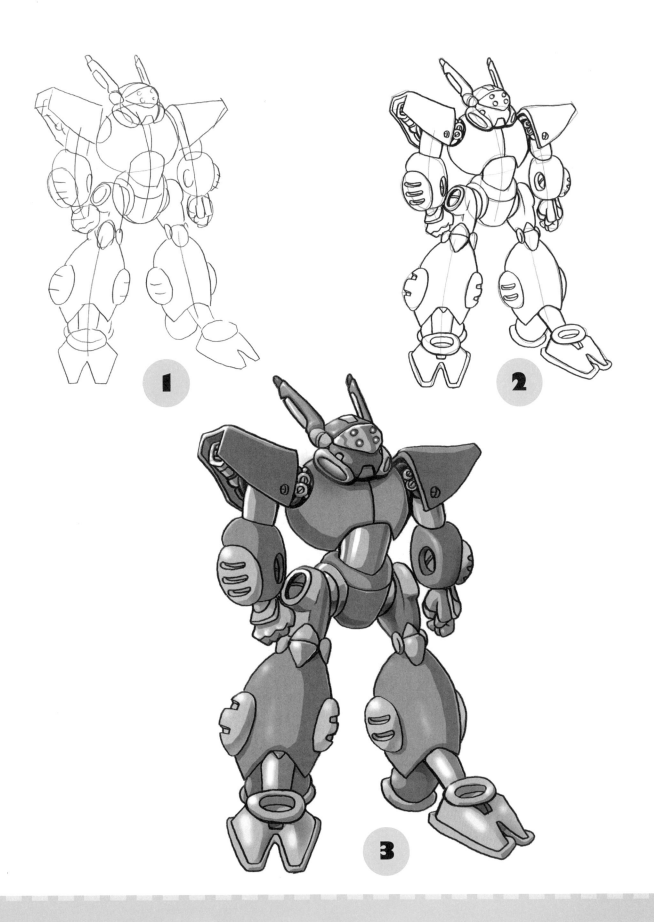

Robot Boy

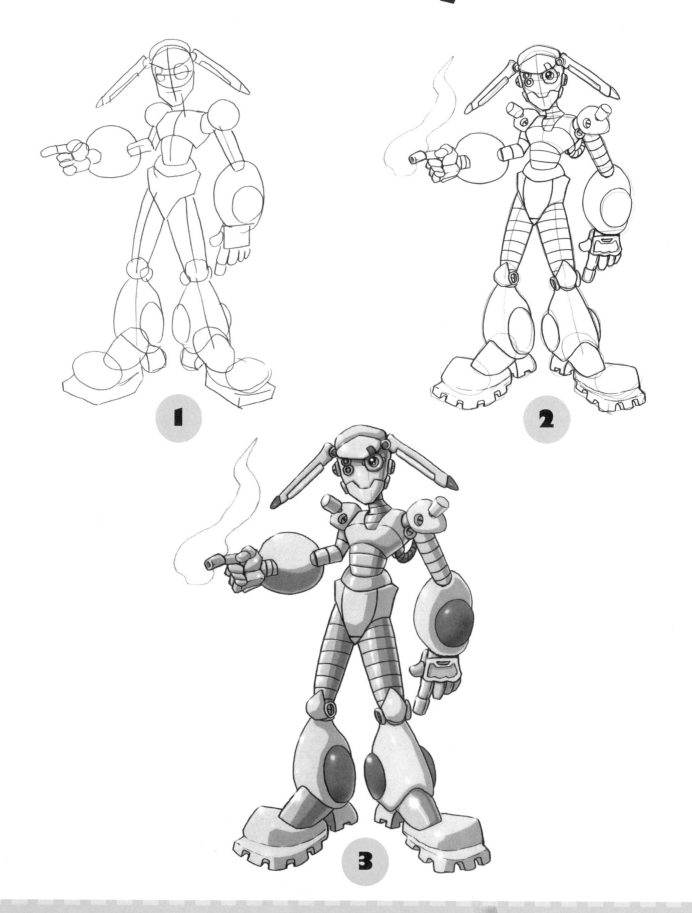

Sporty Car

Flying Car

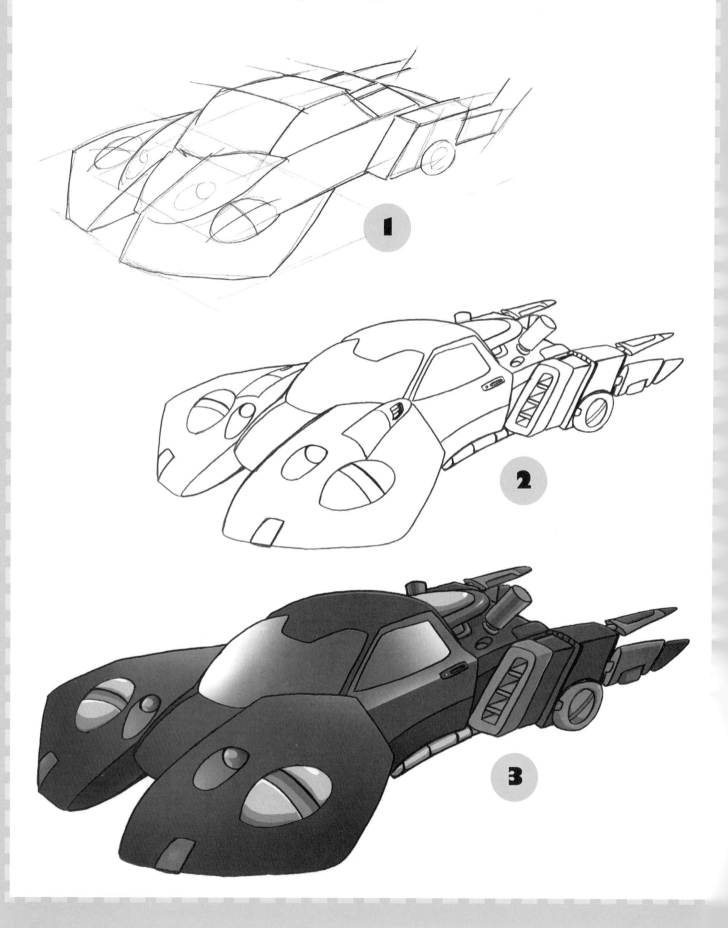

Good Guy Space Fighter

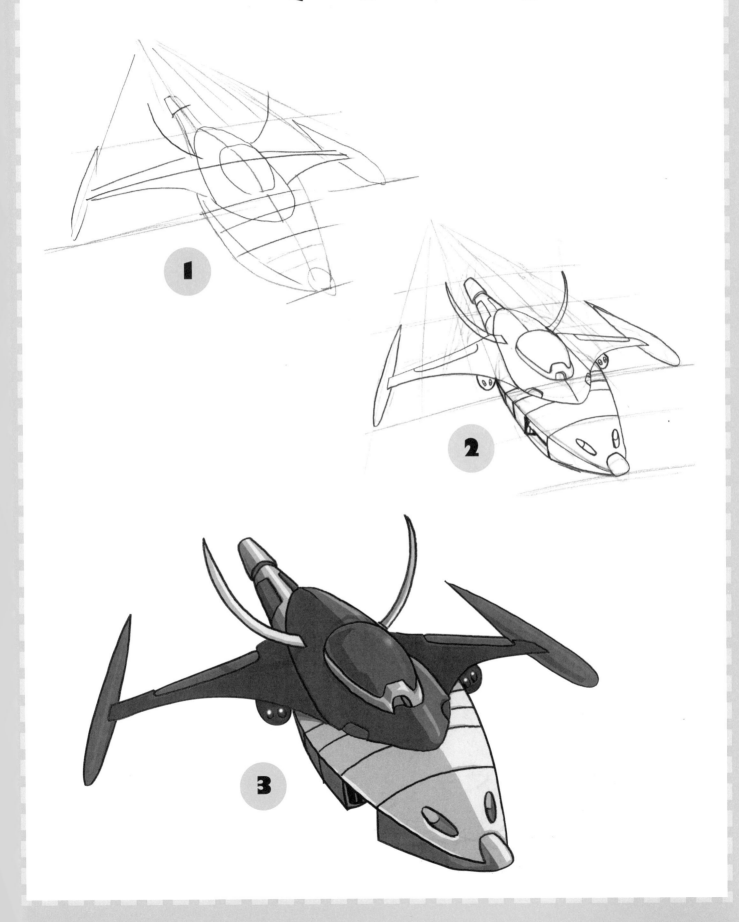

Pirate Space Fighter

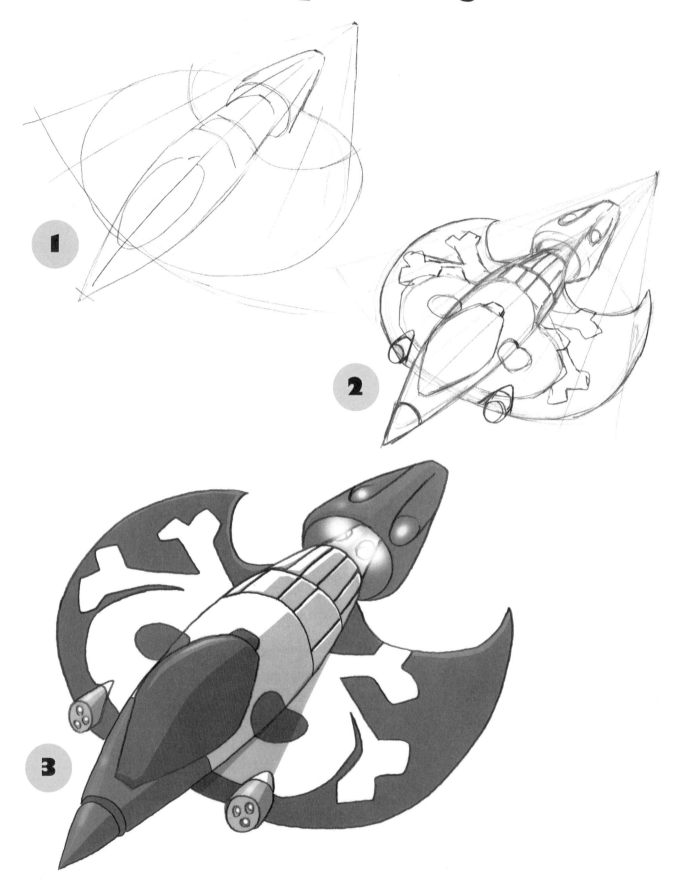

Space Station

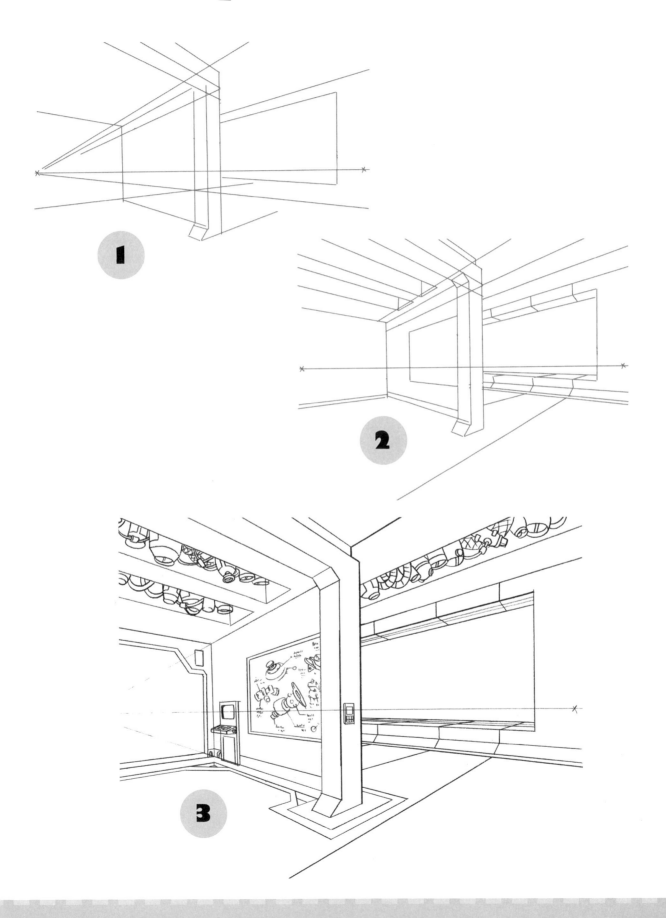

Fantasy Castle

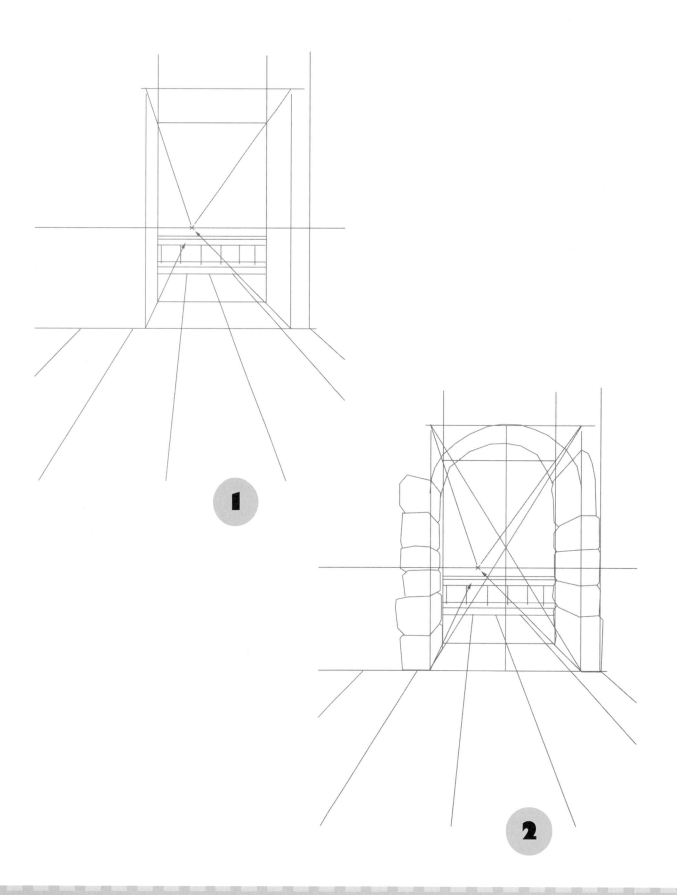

Traditional Japanese Home

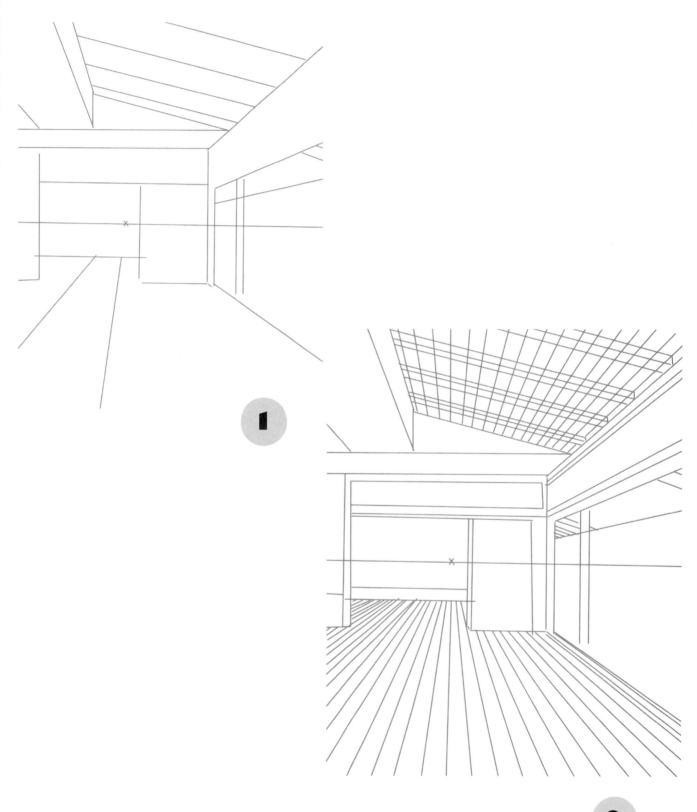

3

City Buildings

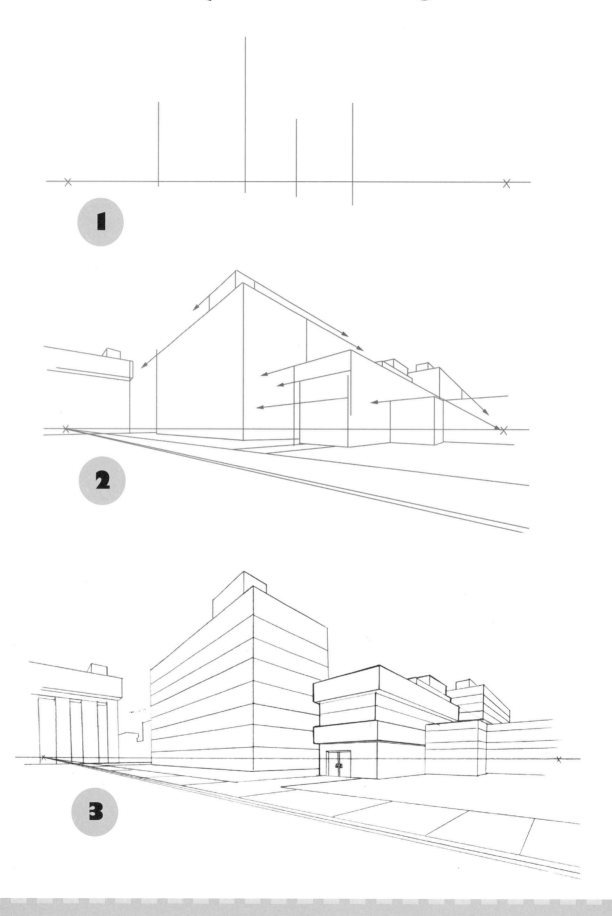

About the Author

David Okum has worked as a freelance artist and illustrator since 1984 and has had his manga work published since 1992, beginning with a story in a Ninja High School anthology published by Antarctic Press. He has since been included in two other Antarctic Press anthologies and several small-press comic books. His writing and artwork have appeared in six books by Guardians of Order, publishers of Big Eyes, Small Mouth (the anime and manga role-playing game).

David studied fine art and history at the University of Waterloo and works as a high school art teacher.

F-W PUBLICATIONS, INC.

Other fine Impact books are available from your local bookstore, art supply store or direct from the publisher.

09 08 07 06 05   5 4 3 2 1

DISTRIBUTED IN CANADA BY FRASER DIRECT
100 Armstrong Avenue
Georgetown, ON, Canada L7G 5S4
Tel: (905) 877-4411

DISTRIBUTED IN THE U.K. AND EUROPE BY DAVID & CHARLES
Brunel House, Newton Abbot, Devon, TQ12 4PU, England
Tel: (+44) 1626 323200, Fax: (+44) 1626 323319
Email: mail@davidandcharles.co.uk

DISTRIBUTED IN AUSTRALIA BY CAPRICORN LINK
P.O. Box 704, S. Windsor NSW, 2756 Australia
Tel: (02) 4577-3555

Library of Congress Cataloging in Publication Data

Okum, David, 1967-
    Draw super manga! / David Okum.— 1st ed.
          p. cm
    ISBN 1-58180-732-5 (pbk. : alk. paper)
    1. Comic books, strips, etc. —Japan—Technique--Juvenile literature. 2. Cartooning—Technique--Juvenile literature. I. Title.

NC1764.5.J3O475 2005
741.5'0952--dc22   2005006214

Editor: Mona Michael
Production editor: Jenny Ziegler
Designer: Wendy Dunning
Production artist: Brian Schroeder
Production coordinator: Mark Griffin

Collect Them All!

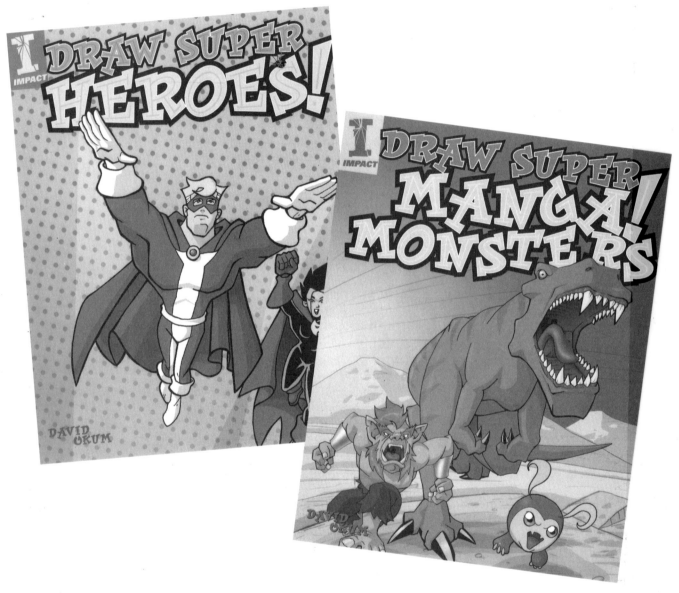

These books and other **IMPACT** titles are available at your local arts &
craft retailer, bookstore, online supplier or by calling 1-800-448-0915
in North America or 0870 2200220 in the United Kingdom.
Visit www.impact-books.com.